Build a Pond for Food & Fun
By D. J. Young

Build a Pond for Food & Fun

By D. J. Young

The farm or homestead fishpond slowly is gaining recognition for what it actually can be: a multi-valued asset. It finally is proving itself; it is proving that it can provide fish and recreation for the entire family, plus some surplus for friends and neighbors; or some surplus to sell, if it is large enough and properly managed. In addition to its primary purpose of raising fish, it can be a source of water for irrigating the garden, the orchard, watering cattle . . . even water for firefighting in case of an emergency.

Many times fishponds have been tried and termed "unproductive—not worth the effort and expense." The reasons for failure can be traced to poor pond construction, based on bad advice or no advice. Productive fishponds are the result of following good and proper planning. Like constructing a home, there are proven, effective designs. Not every house plan will provide the comforts desired; not every fishpond plan will support fish.

Construction expertise in the field of aquaculture lies with the USDA Soil Conservation Service, the US Fish and Wildlife Service, and the fish and wildlife services of the various States.

Regrettably, in spite of this expertise we produce less than 3 percent of our fish needs through aquaculture, while the world output has more than doubled during the past five years. Some countries produce nearly 40 percent of their total needs. We apparently are not taking advantage of one of our natural resources.

With the available expertise, the United States can do as well as the rest of the world; the farm family can do better. It can produce well over 50 percent of its fish needs. This bulletin is designed to help the farm family or homesteader increase that productivity.

Many farms or homesteads have natural ponds that can be converted into productive fishponds. In this bulletin you will find diagrams to show you how this can be done. Other farms have excellent sites for building man-made fishponds. You also will find here plans and suggestions to help you build it right the first time. Productive fishponds are not accidents; they don't just *happen.*

A well planned and constructed fishpond will pay for itself in time. It will add to the economy by furnishing food for the family, as well as providing recreation. It can serve as a pond for fishing, a swimming pool in summer, or as an ice skating rink in winter in northern regions where water freezes to a sufficient thickness. A fishpond, in addition to being a sound and basic instrument of resource management, is a means of improving property value.

Selecting the Site

The most important part of any plan for constructing your fishpond is selecting the proper site. This decision will determine the initial cost, maintenance cost, productivity, utility and life of the pond.

First, you need a basin that will hold water. The best water-holding areas are small depressed valleys or wet land areas that are not suited for crop cultivation. Most such areas will be found to have the necessary water-holding qualities.

If your farm or homestead does not have such areas, make certain that the soil in the site you select will hold water without excess seepage. Unless you are an expert in the field, don't trust your own judgment; it may be a waste of time, effort and money. The Soil Conservation Service is at your service in such matters. It will make the necessary tests, borings, etc., then advise you if the soil at the prospective site has the necessary impervious characteristics.

The use you will make of the pond also should determine the location, where there is a choice of locations. If it is to be used mainly for stocking fish, swimming in summer, or ice skating in winter, it is best located near the home. If it can be located near the home, you may wish to install a dry hydrant for use of the water for fire protection or for irrigating the garden during periods of drought.

The available water supply certainly will be a determining factor in your site location. The best and least expensive water source is from a natural watershed, usually found at the head of depressed valleys or wet areas. Such water sources in most cases will preclude locating the pond near the home. On the other hand, if well water is used, the best choice may be near the home because that is the location of most wells.

Both the quantity and quality of the available water are essential elements that must not be overlooked in your search for an ideal site. If the available water supply is from a natural watershed, it should be sufficient to maintain the necessary water level in the pond; if it is not sufficient, the expense of a supplementary water supply will have to be considered. If the watershed supplies too much water, the topography must offer ways to divert the excess water.

Water should not contain contamination, such as runoffs from barn lots, crop fields where insecticides are most likely used. It should not carry silt from surrounding areas. Silt will be less of a problem if the watershed has a good cover of vegetation. If the watershed does not have vegetation, it would be advisable to wait until a good cover can be grown before building the pond. This would only be practical where all of the region or area contributing water is under the control of the prospective pond builder.

Not all farms or homesteads will have ideal fishpond conditions, but lack of the ideal site does not mean that you cannot build a successful pond. Fishponds can be built on more or less flat lands, even when the ideal water-holding qualities of the soil are not present, and an adequate natural watershed not available. This subject will be covered in a later section.

Clearing the Pond Site

After the pond site has been selected, some cleaning-up of the area will have to be done. The type and extent will vary, depending on whether you are converting an existing pond or small lake into a fishpond, building an excavated pond, or an embankment pond.

The embankment pond will entail the most work. All top soil and vegetation should be scraped off—including the area under the planned embankment—and the top soil set aside for later use, if it is to be used for the embankment.

All trees, shrubs, and brush should be cut from the area and the stumps removed. If there are old tree stumps, they should be pulled out with the other vegetation and hauled away.

In addition to the pond and embankment areas, a strip about 15 or 20 feet back from the landside toe of the embankment should be cleared of trees. If trees, especially deciduous trees, are left too close to the water's edge, the leaves that will fall in the water and decay will rob the pond of oxygen needed by the fish.

The absence of leaves in your pond, in addition to the smooth bottom resulting from the clearing of tree stumps, will ease seining operations, an important part of good pond management.

Where existing ponds or small lakes are being converted into fishponds, or where an excavated pond is being built, it is obvious that much of this cleaning-up will result from the reworking of the existing pond areas, or in the process of excavating, where an excavated pond is being built. However, the embankment site and the 15- or 20-foot strip on the landside toe of the planned embankment should also be cleared, as in the case of the embankment pond. Any organic matter left in the embankment site will cause leaks later as it begins to decay.

Using Existing Ponds or Small Lakes to Build a Fishpond

Many farms will have existing natural ponds or small lakes that can be converted into productive fishponds. Existing ponds or small lakes, in most cases, can be safely assumed to have the necessary water-retaining soil and a sufficient water supply from a natural watershed.

Locations where these natural conditions exist usually produce the most economical and successful fishponds. Such natural water basins will not, however, obviate the necessity of checking the quality of the water supply; it must be free of contamination detrimental to fish. Before proceeding with the pond construction, have your State Game Commissioner, or a private laboratory, make an analysis of the water at its source.

Also, the water source should be sufficient to furnish an adequate supply during droughts, with diversionary waterways to by-pass excess waters during heavy rains. Excess waters should not flow through your pond for reasons of good fish management and maintenance of embankments and spillways.

Existing ponds will, undoubtedly, contain unwanted trash fishes. The first step should be to get rid of them. The chemical rotenone is used for that purpose, but before using rotenone, determine if the existing pond or lake will need to be reworked. Chances are that it will, in which case the best way of ridding it of trash fishes, fish eggs and parasites will be to drain it and let it dry completely. Besides ridding the pond of unwanted fishes, etc., draining and drying the basin will make the reworking chore much simpler.

In reworking an existing pond or small lake, the same principles recommended for building a new pond should be followed. Excavation along the rim, as well as the bottom, will no doubt be necessary, as most ponds or lakes existing for some years will have shallow, silted edges.

The silt must be removed to make the edge of your pond as nearly perpendicular as practical. Shallow edges allow vegetation to grow, which decomposes and depletes the water of oxygen, besides harboring mosquitoes and other insects.

In deepening the pond, the type of fish you plan to stock it with will be a governing factor. This subject will be covered in the following section.

Diagram A shows a situation where a shallow pond is reworked to form a good contour for a successful fishpond. Solid lines show the bottom contour with silted edges. The dotted line shows the newly formed bottom and edge contours. Silt and other soil removed in the excavation process may be used to form an embankment around the pond, except on the watershed side. The embankment immediately should be seeded with sod-forming grass and allowed to settle completely before the pond is filled with water. If that is not done, the embankment will erode back into the pond, forming shallow, silted edges again in a short time.

A good vegetation cover should be maintained on your watershed. Construct a coarse gravel or rock filter bed for your water to run over just before it enters your pond. This has the effect of cleaning and aerating it.

Refer to other diagrams in this bulletin which will demonstrate methods of building embankments and several methods of drainage to meet your particular pond's water control needs.

Not to be overlooked as possible fishpond sites are abandoned sand or gravel pits; or excavations along highway systems, especially the Federal Interstate Highway System. The federal government buys acres of land to excavate for soil needed in building approaches to over-passes. Some of these are abandoned as useless holes, but many landowners have the foresight to pump them full of water and stock them with fish.

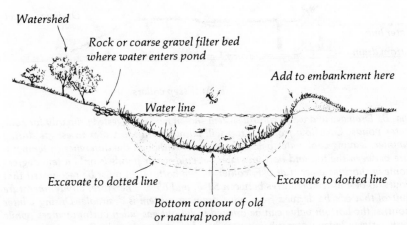

Dia. A. *Converting existing ponds or small lakes into fishponds. Use excavated dirt to build embankment around the pond, except on watershed side. Seed immediately with sod-forming grass to prevent erosion. See other diagrams in this bulletin for instructions on building the embankment and drainage system.*

One disadvantage is that the water cannot be managed by any drainage and supply system except by pumping it in and out. Pumping it out is the major chore when it becomes necessary to clean out the pit for restocking. But when one figures that they have been excavated at no cost to the user, they should not be overlooked. Many have been successfully stocked with fish.

Types of Fishponds

By types of fishponds we mean the type constructed for the particular species of fish that will be stocked in the pond, and not types of ponds constructed for other purposes. Various species of fish do best with certain depths of water and temperature.

For example, trout—rainbow, brook, cutthroat, brown—do best in ponds of 8- to 10-foot depths. Trout ponds are generally classified as cold-water ponds with temperatures ranging between 33°F. in winter to 75°F. in summer. The temperature factor makes the depth necessary. Cold-water ponds need special drainage systems through the embankment. See Diagram B for suggested design and explanation for this type of pond.

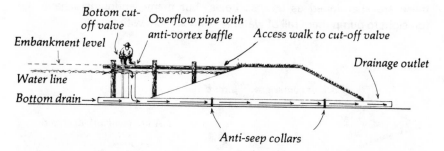

Dia. B. Drainage and water control system shown here is suggested primarily for cold-water ponds. Overflow from the top will allow warm top water to escape during summer, leaving cool water below the surface. Although the difference in temperature between the top and bottom waters in cold-water ponds is only a few degrees (some authorities place it at 6°F. colder on the bottom), it must be recognized that trouts do best at temperatures between 50°F. and 65°F. Therefore, any temperature control that can be derived from your drainage system is desirable. During winter months, the bottom valve can be opened to let out gas-laden bottom waters, while fresh, oxygen-laden water is being introduced from the top under the ice.

In small ponds of one acre or less, this drainage design should be sufficient to control water levels without the additional expense of a spillway if a twelve-inch drainpipe is installed with an anti-vortex baffle so it can handle the maximum volume of water.

Trout in farm fishponds will not reproduce, however. They must be stocked every two or three years for harvesting.

If the water in your pond is too warm for trout—due to climate and geographical location—the best combination to stock is bass with bluegill. They reproduce well in properly managed and fertilized ponds; the bluegills feed on the plankton and micro-organisms promoted by sunlight and fertilization, and the bass feed on the bluegill fingerlings. They are an excellent combination, but the pond must be designed for those species if best results are expected.

The minimum water depths for bass and bluegill during periods of prolonged drought should not be below four feet; the ideal is six feet, with eight feet the maximum depth recommended. The necessity for a dependable water supply control readily can be appreciated.

In some sections of the country catfish ponds are popular. The recommended water depth for this species of fish is 2½ feet on the shallow end of the pond, and 4 to 6 feet on the deep end.

Ponds designed for bass and bluegill or catfish are generally referred to as warm-water ponds. The basic design can be used for both species, with due consideration to the depth requirements of each.

Since ponds designed for both species are classed as warm-water ponds, the drainage and overflow systems are the same, both designed to drain off the cool bottom water and retain warm top water. (See Diagram C and text for suggested systems and reasons for modifications under various conditions.)

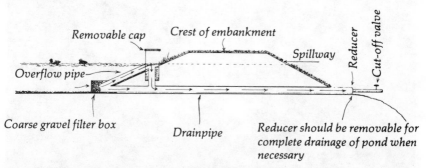

Dia. C. Drainage and water control system shown here is suggested for warm-water fishponds. It draws cold water from the bottom of the pond and avoids loss of warm top-water, helping to warm the pond in the spring. The sleeve over the overflow pipe prevents small fish from escaping. Drainage design assumes an abrupt land-fall on the landside of the pond. This condition will not prevail in all cases; therefore, it may be necessary to extend the drainpipe underground for some distance to the nearest land-fall.

Some modification of this drainage design should be made as conditions dictate. A gatevalve should be installed between the top-water outlet and the bottom-water outlet so a control of outlets exists. (See Dia. B.) Also, if the water is not to be used for irrigation or watering cattle through a reduced outlet, but just dumped in a passing waterway, a standpipe should be installed with its maximum height about three inches below that of the overflow pipe in the pond. This standpipe prevents fish from escaping while letting water out from the bottom outlet. (See photo 1.)

It can be further modified to let the reducer remain to control water for irrigation and cattle-watering in combination with the standpipe to take care of excess waters during heavy rains. By installing the standpipe on a tee between the embankment and the reducer, the upright length can be lowered when it becomes necessary to drain the pond. This helps achieve maximum flexibility in your drainage system.

Photo 1. Two six-inch standpipes are shown here on the drain side of a two-pond complex. The pipes are three inches shorter than the overflow pipe in the pond. They take care of excess waters from rain and from the replenishing water system. The standpipe is built on a tee; the upright end can be lowered if pond drainage is necessary. The size of the pipe is governed by the size of the pond.

Constructing New Fishponds
(The Excavated Pond)

New ponds come in two categories: the excavated pond and the embankment pond.

Excavated ponds are generally regarded as the simpler and the more economical to build on nearly level land. Excavated ponds eliminate the need for expensive and elaborate embankments, spillways, and drainage systems. Their maintenance cost is low, and they are relatively safe from flood water damages. Their disadvantage may be in the size limitations of the area that can be excavated.

Conditions outlined in the chapter on site selection should be observed when selecting a site, especially the water-holding capacity of the soil. Test borings to the proposed depth of the pond, then filling the hole with water, will give some idea of the water-holding capacity of the lower soil strata. If there is some doubt that the test reflects the bottom strata, set a pipe the full depth of the hole, then fill the pipe with water. This will assure you that the test reflects the water-holding capacity of the soil at the maximum proposed depth of the pond and not of the soil on the way down the hole.

Excavated ponds fall into three categories, based on their water sources: (1) the pond fed by surface runoffs, (2) the pond fed by ground water aquifers, and (3) the pond fed by underground water from natural springs or water pumped from man-made wells.

The pond fed by surface water resembles the embankment pond in that respect. Surface runoff is the most economical source of water, but must be sufficient to maintain the desired water depth or a supplementary source should be provided. Provisions for diversion of excess waters also must be included in the overall construction plan. Excess or flood waters must not be allowed to run through the pond.

Ponds that are fed by ground water aquifers can be located only in relatively flat areas, and where the water table is within a few feet of the surface. The same borings that can determine the water-holding qualities of your soil at the pond site will show the level of the water table.

Naturally, if you have a good water table, the water-holding qualities of the soil at the pond site will not be a problem; should your water table be too low, plans for a supplementary water supply should be included in your pond plans.

And, your choice of pond site may have neither surface runoff waters nor ground water aquifers. This need not be a deterring factor; many successful ponds are built and fed by spring water or by underground water pumped from man-made wells. The initial cost of water from a man-made well will be higher, but maintaining the necessary water level in the pond will be relatively easy to control, and inexpensive, if your soil has good water-holding qualities.

Well water is thought to be best by many fishpond owners and many authorities. It is not muddy, has no unwanted fish, nor does it contain chemicals often found in runoff waters. A disadvantage is that such waters often contain dissolved carbon dioxide or nitrogen, at the same time lacking oxygen—a situation deadly to fish. This condition is simple to correct by splashing the well water over baffles or running it through a bed of coarse gravel or stones, or splashing it through the air in a fall of four to six feet. (See photo no. 2.)

The life and success of your fishpond will depend largely on its ability to retain the desired water level. Should the water to your pond site be from surface runoff or from natural springs or pumped from man-made wells and should there also be some doubt that the soil has the necessary water-holding qualities, consult your Soil Conservation Commissioner about the use of bentonite as a sealing agent.

Bentonite is a volcanic clay that is an excellent sealing compound. It is applied by mixing about two pounds per square foot of land surface, discing it into the top six inches of soil, then packing it tightly. When wet, it will swell to several times its original volume, forming a good seal. (See photos No. 3 & 3A.)

Photo 2. *Underground water being splashed through the air before entering the pond. This procedure adds oxygen to the water.*

Photo 3. Working bentonite into the soil in bottom of pond with rototiller. Soil was tilled to five-inch depth. (USDA-SCS photograph)

Photo 3-A. Bentonite being disced into bottom of reservoir; sheepsfoot being used to compact the soil after the sealing agent is mixed with the soil. (USDA-SCS photograph)

The shape of excavated ponds is somewhat limited. The rectangular ponds are the most popular because they are simpler to build and can be adapted to most kinds of excavating equipment. The width will be dictated by the size of the excavating equipment available, mainly the boom of the dragline excavator; the length by the square feet of water surface desired. To obtain the maximum amount of water surface desired, it is sometimes best to consider building two or more ponds side by side with driveways between the ponds. (See photo No. 4.)

Photo 4. *To obtain the maximum amount of surface water, it is best to build two or more ponds side by side with driveways between each pond. Shown here are two such ponds, each with about three acres of surface water.*

Diagram D presupposes an excavated, square-shaped pond with a land-fall immediately near the pond. This situation is ideal and will not occur often. In other than ideal situations the drainage system will not apply and provisions for pumping out the water will have to be included so the pond can be drained when the need arises.

The slope and catch basin design should be followed, regardless of the drainage system. It may be necessary to drain the pond to rid it of trash fish or parasites. The advantages of the slopes and catch basin will then become evident—and will be direly missed if not included in the original construction.

The diagram also presupposes that the excavated material will be used at the site of the pond for building an embankment around the excavated area, increasing the water depth.

Some authorities recommend hauling away the excavated material. This is an expensive procedure. Ponds have been observed where the excavated soil was placed to good use building embankments around the excavated area to raise the water level of the pond. (See Photo No. 4.) This procedure reduces the amount of excavation necessary to achieve the desired depth. The only material that should be hauled away is the topsoil and vegetation excavated from the pond area, including the area where the embankment will be constructed.

When an embankment is built around an excavated pond, the three steps outlined in Diagram E should be followed. In addition the foot of the embankment on the water side of the pond should be set about three feet from the edge of the excavation, leaving a narrow path or ledge—referred to as a berm—between the embankment and the water's edge. This berm will keep the soil of the embankment from washing into the pond.

Where an embankment is built around an excavated pond, a drainage system should be installed to the level of the outside land-fall. This probably will not be to the level of the bottom water level of the pond, but it will help drainage when that chore becomes necessary, and will take care of overflow problems caused by heavy rains. Choose the drainage system that applies to your particular type pond (Diagrams B and C), then supplement it with a centrifugal pump, if necessary.

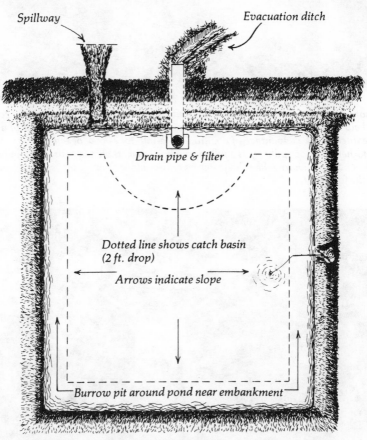

Dia. D. A 1:3 pond should be built more or less square. If small, oblong ponds are built, the axis should be parallel to the wind to get aeration benefits from the wind action. The reverse is true where long, oblong ponds are built, as wave action is likely to cause erosion problems on the windward side of the pond.

A catch basin should be constructed at the drainpipe, as it may be necessary at times to completely drain the pond to rid it of trash fish or parasites. The catch basin facilitates that chore.

Photo 5. Photo shows section of a pond of about 2 acres; spillways are concrete to help control soil erosion. One four-foot wide spillway, built at the end of a drainage ditch to take advantage of a natural land-fall, takes care of minor excess waters. Another six-foot spillway is built six inches lower than the four-foot spillway; it takes over the chore when the water level rises more than six inches above the level of the four-footer.

Photo 6. Four-foot spillway serving the pond in photo 5 shown handling minor excess water. Note erosion in the area of the spillway, one can visualize the erosion problem if the spillway were not constructed of concrete.

Spillways must be built in the embankment on the down slope side of your pond. The top of the spillway should be two feet below the top of the embankment and wide enough to take care of overflow without creating an erosion problem. In small ponds of one or two acres it is advisable to surface the spillway with concrete to prevent erosion. (See photo Nos. 5-6.)

This particular pond has two concrete spillways, one four feet wide and one six feet wide. The six-foot wide spillway is about six inches higher than the four-foot spillway. When water reaches six inches in depth in the smaller spillway, the larger one takes over part of the chore.

The size of your pond will depend on how you plan to use it. Assuming that it is more or less an exclusive fishpond, then the species of fish you plan to stock it with will be a factor.

Trout ponds smaller than one-half to one acre will not provide sufficient fishing for your family and some friends. Ponds from one to three acres are more satisfactory. While well-designed ponds ranging to as much as twenty acres are not an exception, a series of smaller ponds may be more manageable if that much fishing area is desired.

Bass and bluegill ponds should be one acre or more. Smaller ponds will not produce enough fish for good weekly catches, making it necessary to restock frequently.

Catfish can be raised in ponds smaller than one acre. Like trout, they will not reproduce satisfactorily under ordinary farm pond conditions; they have to be restocked for harvesting and fed on a regular schedule. Ponds of one acre or over will provide more fishing enjoyment.

If ponds are to be used for other purposes, such as garden irrigation or cattle watering, consideration of that water need should be included in your overall pond plans.

Construction of New Ponds (The Embankment Pond)

Embankment ponds are the most expensive and difficult to build. You will, no doubt, need an engineer or some other expert technical advice and assistance in both the planning and construction phases.

Elevation of dams and spillways will have to be calculated precisely; the exact degrees of slope in the pond as well as of the spillway will have to be determined. The impervious nature of the soil at the depth of excavation; the suitability of material for building the dam; the best type of sealing agent for the particular condition—all these factors have to be expertly planned and executed. A poorly planned embankment pond, even one that is well planned but poorly constructed, will not only be a sore disappointment but a waste of money.

More heavy equipment is needed for embankment ponds than for any other type of pond. This equipment may include a dragline excavator, bulldozer, tractor-pulled wheeled scraper, sheepsfoot roller and a compaction roller. Renting this type of equipment can be expensive; if you have to hire the operators, it will add to the cost substantially. The extent of the equipment requirement and its use will, of course, depend on the size of the pond.

Before making even the initial plans for an embankment pond, you should contact the Soil Conservation people. They provide many free services in the planning and construction phases; an engineer's assistance may be needed in addition.

Embankment ponds usually are built in valleys at the foot of a watershed, or at the foot of a small stream. Care should be taken about interrupting normal waterflows that affect other farms in the area. Check with your county and state authorities before altering streams, regardless of how small. The red tape involved in harnessing some stream waters is so involved that most times it is not worth the effort.

The solution might be to build your pond on the edge of a stream, then pump the water into the pond. However, such stream waters, commonly referred to as "wild waters," may be rife with trash fish that you will not want in your pond. Provisions will have to be made to eliminate these unwanted fish from your water. The only known way to remove wild fish and fish eggs from stream water is to pass the water through a saran or fiberglass screen filter, mesh size 907.

This filtration should be made for the initial filling of the pond and during periodic replenishing. For the initial filling, besides filtering, it is recommended that wild water be treated with rotenone before stocking. The following recommendations for use of rotenone with wild water before stocking of fish was made by the U.S. Fish and Wildlife Service.

Treat wild water with three quarts of five percent liquid rotenone, or six pounds of five percent powder, per acre-foot of water. An acre-foot is the surface area of your pond times the depth in feet. Water temperature at the time of treatment should be between 70° and 80°F. Wait a minimum of thirty days before stocking.

Building the Embankment and Spillway— Installing Drainpipe

After the suitability of the site has been established, the next most important factor is the foundation under the embankment. It must assure stability for the structure and be resistant to water seepage.

The soil stratum under the embankment must be closely studied. If it is of such nature that it will not hold water satisfactorily, the cut-off core under the embankment must be rendered leak-proof with bentonite or other sealing agent. Even the core of the embankment may need to be sealed with leak-proofing material.

Refer to Diagram E for instructions on the steps necessary to build a well-structured embankment. The depth and width of the cut-off core (first step) will depend on the size of the pond. The dimensions given on the diagram are considered minimum.

A core should continue to the height of the embankment and consist of the same leak-proof material that the cut-off core was constructed with— impervious clay, well compacted, or other soils mixed with a sealing agent. Both the water and land sides of the embankment can be finished with other soil types that will compact reasonably well.

The *minimum* slopes are as indicated, with the landside and waterside turfed to prevent erosion. If the soil available to finish the embankment is coarse-textured, gravelly and sandy, no doubt the Soil Conservation Service will recommend use of a sealing agent on the waterside surface of the embankment. This would prevent it from later eroding into the pond.

The slope of the embankment on the waterside can vary as much as 1½:1, if the soil is clayey enough to withstand erosion, but with sandy or gravelly soils the 3:1 is advisable. Vegetation problems will have to be coped with as they occur.

Lay the drainpipe after the cut-off core is built and before the embankment core is built. The size will depend on the size of the pond. This is something that your engineer can figure out, based on your pond's water volume. The outlet system inside the pond will depend on the type of pond you are building. Refer back to the section on types of ponds and Diagrams B and C for guidance.

In addition to the drainage pipe installed with the appropriate overflow pipe on the inside, a substantially built spillway is essential. It must be designed to take care of major overflows that might occur during heavy rains, spring melting snows or storms.

The spillway dimensions shown in Diagram E are considered minimum for a small pond of one to two acres. It should be level—true to the water level in the pond—so that more water will not spill over on one side than the other, starting an eroding condition. It should be at least well turfed, but it is strongly recommended that concrete be used, to obviate any danger of erosion. (See photo No. 6.)

1st Step

Arrows indicate ground level

Dia. E. Start building the embankment around your fishpond by excavating a trench deep enough to remove the top soil, and about 4 feet wide, then fill with impervious material, such as clay, compacting it well by layers.

2nd Step

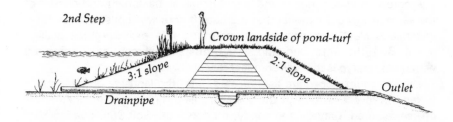

Crown landside of pond-turf

3:1 slope   2:1 slope

Drainpipe   Outlet

Continue building the embankment core with clay up to the crown. Complete building sides with other soils, but not extremely sandy or gravelly soil. The soil removed in excavating the pond should be sufficient to build the embankment. If clay is not available in your area, see text on the use of bentonite, a volcanic clay, to arrest seepage.

3rd Step

Turf spillway 2 ft. below top of embankment, at least 10 ft. wide.

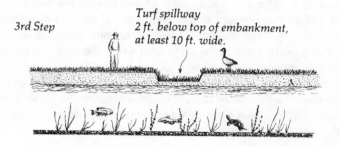

Water—The Life of Your Pond

It would be elementary to say that without water you would have no fishpond. It is just as elementary to say that without *good* water—water with the needed qualities and devoid of harmful properties—you will have no fishpond. A pond—but without fish.

If water is the life of your pond, there must be a sufficient supply. Your water supply should be capable of replacing its volume in one year—water lost through evaporation and runoffs. Added to that volume must be water intended for other uses, such as garden irrigation or cattle watering, and periodic drainage of some bottom waters, especially in cold regions where the water freezes over for prolonged periods.

The source of this water can be natural runoff from a watershed, spring or well water, or "wild water" pumped in from nearby streams. Its source is not as important as its quality and quantity.

Underground waters, whether from springs, artesian wells or man-made wells, contain dissolved carbon dioxide, nitrogen and iron, all lethal to fish, and have very little oxygen, which is essential to fish life.

The carbon dioxide can be eliminated from such waters, and oxygen added, by aeration. This can be accomplished by running it over baffles or through a bed of rocks or stones, or just spraying it in the air four to six feet.

"Wild water" from streams can be risky water. Before planning a fishpond with that source of water in mind, investigate the stream's tributaries. If the water comes from cultivated fields you must be cautious about harmful chemicals. Have a sample tested by a reliable laboratory. If it is free of harmful chemicals, filter as recommended in the chapter on building an embankment pond, to keep out trash fish.

Wild water is often muddy. If it is too muddy it will silt your pond in a short time. Besides, muddy water is not conducive to good fish growth. It reduces the potential for oxygen production and retention, and excludes the sunlight necessary for the growth and reproduction of fish food organisms.

Natural food reproduction in your pond waters is important and necessary, regardless of the practice of feeding with commercial fish foods, especially where bass and bluegill are stocked. The bluegill feed on the plankton and organisms promoted by sunlight and oxygen; the bass in turn feed on the bluegill fingerlings.

Muddy water, however, may not be entirely objectionable; it is impractical to expect crystal-clear water, unless it originates from underground springs. Muddiness can result from large amounts of suspended clay particles. It surely will be present right after construction activities and before vegetation has time to grow on surrounding embankments.

Muddy water containing suspended particles of soil can be cleared by treating with gypsum at the rate of 12 to 35 pounds per 1,000 cubic feet of water, or 30 to 50 pounds of aluminum sulphate per acre-foot of water. (One acre-foot of water equals 43,560 cubic feet.) Some pond operators report good clearing results with the use of 8-8-8 commercial fertilizer.

The amount of treating material applied to your pond waters will depend on the degree of turbidity. It would be wise to get expert advice from your Soil Conservation or State Game Commission before undertaking any water treatment with the chemicals mentioned above.

Water quality should be maintained at its source after the initial filling of your pond. It is more economical and wiser to *maintain* its quality at the source than having to *correct* it after the water has reached your pond. This applies particularly to ponds fed by watershed waters.

Photo 7. An ideal embankment pond situation with a natural watershed. Note vegetation growing in the normal water course, a desirable condition which has the effect of cleaning muddy waters before they reach the pond. (USDA-SCS photograph)

Photo 8. The embankment of an embankment pond, well turfed to prevent erosion. The trickle or overflow pipe is set in the water side toe of the embankment. This is desirable in regions where water freezes for prolonged periods. Board on top of overflow pipe serves as anti-vortex baffle. (USDA-SCS photograph)

A good vegetation cover on your watershed will prevent the soil from eroding into your pond, causing muddy waters. If your watershed provides too much water, the vegetation will retain the water long enough to give some of it time to soak into the ground. If there is still an excess, a diversion ditch may be necessary to divert it away from your pond. Too much water coursing through your pond may carry fertilizer with it, making it difficult to maintain the quality of water desired.

Arrange to keep cattle away from your pond. Cattle trampling around the edges will muddy your water. If you have cattle you want to benefit from the waters of your pond—and that is certainly a good conservation practice —fence the pond and pipe the overflow waters from your trickle system to nearby cattle watering facilities.

Ducks and geese are pretty in a pond, but if you want to use the pond for swimming, you will not find the condition they create compatible with swimming activities. If your pond is for fish only, a few ducks and geese will not affect the condition of your water; too many will.

Temperature As a Water Condition

Temperature is a water condition—and a most important one, depending on the species of fish you will stock.

If you plan a trout pond, temperatures should range between 33° F. (the temperature just below the ice in winter) to 75° F. Trout show their most rapid growth in waters with temperature ranges between 50° F. and 65° F., but it is not likely that this range can be maintained throughout the year.

If the temperature of your water source and your general climate does not allow you to maintain an acceptable trout-pond temperature, you may wish to stock bass and bluegill, or catfish. The temperature for these species of fish range from 80° F. to 90° F. or higher, measured a few inches below the surface.

Photo 9. An ideal embankment pond site. Clearing of area has begun; fences are being erected to keep cattle away. Area extends to the rear line of trees. It eventually will furnish about three acres of good fishing.

Water temperatures ranging between the two extremes just cited are too warm for trout and too cold for warm-water fish. Such temperatures usually range from 70° F. to 80° F. Ponds with these temperature ranges are common in some sections of the North, mid-West and at high altitudes.

There is no practical way to make a pond colder, but you can raise your pond water temperature by routing the in-flow of water along the bottom of your pond and the overflow out through the bottom trickle and drainage system. This allows the warm water to remain on top. (See Diagrams B and C.) Bottom drainage devices should be installed in all ponds.

Oxygen and pH As a Water Condition

Oxygen content is an essential quality of your pond water. All animal life in your pond uses it twenty four hours per day. The oxygen content should be at least five parts per million.

The acidity-alkalinity level of the water you use in your pond is as important as any other condition of your water. Growth and reproduction of fish is best with a pH of 7 or 9; 4.0 or lower is lethal to fish. Moderate acidity can be corrected by adding agricultural limestone to the water. Your pond water should be tested; then you should proceed to correct any acidity-alkalinity problems under expert supervision.

Your Soil Conservation Service and Other Government Agencies

What help can you expect from your Soil Conservation Service? They will not build your pond, nor will they bear any of the cost.

Your local Soil Conservation representative, however, will give the assistance you may need in planning your pond, aid in selecting the site, assist in meeting your water needs, help design your pond, and work with your contractor. Soil conservation is his business, and anything that has to do with better use of soil and water comes under that heading. You will find him most cooperative.

Included in your plan for a fishpond must be the species of fish you want to stock in it, and its availability. Contact your State Game Commission and the United States Fish and Wildlife Service. They have representatives near you; consult with them and heed their advice. Those two agencies are there to serve you.

State and Federal Laws

Not all states have laws regulating home fishponds, but some do. Check with your State Game Commission. Also, some states have water authorities that regulate the use of water. Don't overlook them. Your local Soil Conservation representative is well posted on these matters; he can direct you to the specific authorities. Learn what you can or cannot do before you get started.

There is probably nothing in your particular locale that would prevent you from building your fishpond. There are probably just a few regulations you will have to comply with. But initial compliance with regulations can save future difficulties.

Photo 10. The overflow pipe inside the pond with cut-off valve controlling flow of bottom waters. (See Diagram B.) Walkway leads from embankment to the overflow and cut-off system for servicing.

Photo 11. *Twelve-inch standpipe, sufficient to take care of water overflowing from a drainpipe the size shown in photo 10. Such large standpipes are sometimes used in small ponds in lieu of a spillway. With an anti-vortex baffle at the overflow intake, it will handle considerable water, as is evident in this photo. (USDA-SCS photograph)*

Photo 12. *Section of a 2 acre suburban fishpond, showing the tranquility and beauty surrounding it on a peaceful afternoon. The few ducks add beauty to the pond and do no harm if the pond is not intended for swimming.*

Values of a Fishpond

Fishing is an American heritage, and the home fishpond has its own realm in that heritage.

A fishpond is a source of food; a well managed fishpond can produce from 400 to 600 pounds of fish per acre per year, enough for family and friends.

The act of fishing, fish cook-outs and good eating, enjoyed by all Americans, are products of a successful fishpond.

The fishpond can provide other types of recreation, such as swimming and canoeing, and in the winter where ice forms solidly enough, you can have your own ice skating rink.

It can add beauty to the homestead; a well managed fishpond can be just as enhancing to a home area as a swimming pool.

You may never want to sell your farm or homestead, but if you ever do, you'll find that your fishpond will increase your property value to equal or surpass the expense of building it. You will find your fishpond to be a total asset.

Photo 13. Elderly farm couple enjoying fishing in their private fishpond. (USDA-SCS photograph)

Photo 14. Canoeing is one of the pleasures that can derive from a farm fishpond. (USDA-SCS photograph)